Indians and the Old West

THE STORY OF THE
FIRST AMERICANS

adapted from the pages
of AMERICAN HERITAGE,
The Magazine of History

by Anne Terry White

SIMON AND SCHUSTER
NEW YORK

The First Americans

Glaciers still blanketed the country when the first Americans—those people who would one day be called Indians—crossed over the land bridges into Alaska. Skirting the ice, they moved slowly down the continent, following the caribou. They discovered the mountains, the rivers, the lakes; they found the forests, the plains, and the deserts. They came always in small groups. But group followed group until, increasing greatly over thousands of years, they peopled the twin continents from the Arctic to the Polar Sea, from the Pacific to the Atlantic.

When white men came to North America, they found the Indians everywhere, and it seemed that there were a great many of them. But actually in all the area that is now the United States, there were only about a million. Strangely, these Indians belonged to many different tribes and spoke a great variety of languages. The Indians had been here so long and had been so separated, one group from another, that north of Mexico alone 500 different dialects were spoken. Some languages were as far apart as English and French. Tribes living side by side sometimes could talk to each other only in sign language.

The first white men in Virginia observed the Indians with great curiosity and wrote detailed reports about them. For Europeans were as eager to hear about the people of the New World as though they were indeed the inhabitants of another planet. One of the things that astonished the white men was Indian farming. The people had maize, a giant grain that was not sown broadcast like wheat or barley but was planted in hills and rows. An Indian word, maize later became known as Indian corn. The Indians also had beans unlike any known in the Old World, and squashes and pumpkins, and a plant called tobacco which they smoked in long pipes.

◄ *A Minnetaree chieftain leading the ceremonial Dog Dance.*

INDIAN TRIBES
IN NORTH AMERICA

*This map shows where
the Indian tribes lived in
1650.*

In the Northeast were
the Iroquois tribes—the
Mohawks, the Senecas,
the Oneidas, Onondagas,
and Cayugas. Here also,
and further south, too,
were Algonkin towns. In
the Southeast were the
Shawnee, Chickasaws,
the Cherokees, and the
Upper and Lower Creeks.

North of the Great
Lakes were the Chippe-
wa and Ottawa tribes.
West of the Mississippi
were the Dakotas — the
Cheyennes, the Sioux,
Apache and Pawnee. The
Mandans lived here, too.

Around the Rockies
were the Utes, the Co-
manche, and the Arapaho
tribes. In New Mexico
and Arizona the Nava-
hos, Zuñi, Hopi, and
Apaches lived. The Nez
Percés lived in Idaho and
the Cayuse in Oregon.

All these, and many
others lived in North
America, when white
men first came to this
country.

WESTERN CREE   EASTERN CREE   ESKIMO

CHIPPEWA   MONTAGNAIS

NORTHEAST HUNTERS

MAINE
MALECITE

PASSAMAQUODDY
PENOBSCOT

ASSINIBOIN

MINNESOTA

HIDATSA

NORTH DAKOTA

TETON
DAKOTA

YANKTON-
DAKOTA

SANTEE
DAKOTA

WISCONSIN

MICH.

CHIPPEWA

CHIPPEWA

OTTAWA

ALGONKIN

VT.

ABNAKI

N.H.

MOHAWK
ONEIDA
ONONDAGA
CAYUGA
SENECA

IROQUOIS

PENNACOOK

MASSACHUSET

MIGMAC

PENOBSCOT

MANDAN

SUTAIO

CHEYENNE

ARIKARA

SOUTH DAKOTA

NEBRASKA

MENOMINEE

FOX SAUK

WINNEBAGO

MICHIGAN

POTAWATOMI

HURON

TOBACCO
NATION

NEUTRALS

NEW YORK

MUNSEE

MAHICAN
PEQUOT

WAMPANOAG
NARRAGANSET

MONTAUK

IOWA

KICKAPOO

MIAMI

ERIE

PENNSYLVANIA

N.J.

DELAWARE

WESTERN FARMERS

IOWA

ILLINOIS

INDIANA

OHIO

NORTHEAST

SUSQUEHANNA

PONCA

OMAHA

OTO

MISSOURI

MD.

NANTICOKE

PAWNEE

KANSAS

MISSOURI

ILLINOIS

HONIASONT

WEST
VIRGINIA

MOSOPELEA

MONETON

VIRGINIA

POWHATAN

KANSAS

MISSOURI

KENTUCKY

MONACAN

SAPONI

TUTELO

PAMLICO

PADUCAH
APACHE

OKLAHOMA

OSAGE

SHAWNEE

NORTH CAROLINA

ENO NOTTOWAY

TUSCARORA

TEXAS

ARKANSAS

TENNESSEE

KASKINAMPO

CHEROKEE

CHERAW

S. CAROLINA

CATAWBA

WICHITA

TAWAKONI

TRIBES

MISSISSIPPI

YUCHI YUCHI

GEORGIA

WATEREE

SANTEE

WACCAMAW

YAMASI

KICHAI

QUAPAW

CHICKASAW

UPPER
CREEKS

ALABAMA

SOUTHEAST

KOASATI

GUALE

COMBAHEE

HASINAI

CADDO

TUNICA

YAZOO

KOROA

CHOCTAW

ALABAMA

LOWER CREEKS

HITCHITI

LIPAN
APACHE

TAENSA

NATCHEZ

BILOXI

APALACHEE

FLORIDA

ATAKAPA

LOUISIANA

TIMUCUA

TONKAWAN
TRIBES

CHITIMACHA

AIS

BOSO

COAPUILTECO

KARANKAWA

CALUSA

TEKESTA

LAGUNERO

CO HUICHOL

PAME

TAMAULIPECO

(ARAWAK)

7

The white men didn't know that these far-wanderers, who had come from Asia bringing with them only the arts of hunting and of chipping stone into weapons and tools, had become the most original and remarkable farmers in the world. The Indians probably developed maize from two or more wild grasses, and through the centuries had produced the five main types of corn: flint, flour, dent, pop, and sweet. In Peru, several varieties of the nightshade plant, including the poisonous jimson weed (or stinkweed), and tobacco, had been crossed with other plants to produce the potato. The Europeans saw only a few of the twenty or more food plants the Indians had discovered and developed, but they were greatly impressed.

When, in 1590, John White painted a picture of an Algonkin "town" in Virginia, he made much of the farming. He drew fields of ripe corn, with an Indian sitting on a sheltered platform to scare the birds away by his continual shouting. He put in a field of young corn to show the manner of planting it in rows and hills. Edging it, he drew a field of pumpkins. He showed tobacco and sunflowers growing. But, of course, he couldn't leave out the fact that the Indians were hunters, too. So he had them shooting deer right in the town.

In every region the white men found the people of the New World living differently, dressing differently, and building different kinds of houses. In rocky New England the Pilgrims saw no towns. For the Algonkins of the northeast woodlands were mainly deer hunters, and deer were too scarce to feed a large population. The woodland Indians had to live in small bands, and their villages of dome-shaped or cone-shaped pole wigwams covered with bark were ramshackle affairs. But these tribes, and others like them east of the Mississippi had birchbark canoes. No other people had such a beautiful boat, so light that a single man could carry it from water to water.

◄ *Colonists found that Indians were expert farmers. In the engraving opposite, the artist has shown fields of corn, in several stages of growth, and pumpkins, planted by an Algonkin tribe.*

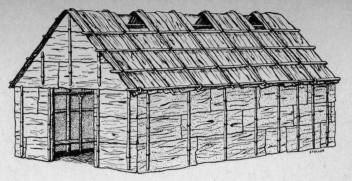

An Iroquois Long House.

The cruel and warlike Iroquois of New York, Pennsylvania and Ohio were a much more formidable group of tribes. They built tight little villages behind strong wooden stockades. Their houses, shaped like Quonset huts, were about 100 feet long, with a row of fires down the middle and a smoke hole over each. Many families of the same clan lived together, every family with its own fireplace and its own quarters. "People of the Longhouse," the Iroquois called themselves.

In the Southeast the Indians built houses to suit the weather. Thus, in Florida a house was just a platform with a thatched roof over it. As for clothes, neither men nor women wore very much although the Indians of the Southeast wove a fine cloth out of plant fibers.

A breechcloth, a bit of skirt, ornaments—that was enough. The men tattooed their bodies, and the greater a warrior was, the more tattooing he had. The hair-do also was extremely important. The men fussed over

The interior of a Long House showing how each family had its own fire.

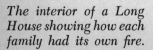

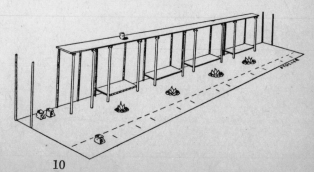

10

their hair, shaving it off or pulling it out in various patterns. But they always left a scalp lock. It was meant as a sort of dare. The lock as much as said, "Come and get me if you can!"

Here in the Southeast the Indians lived by farming and hunting, and they lived very well. But war was the most important affair, to them. It wasn't that they wanted to conquer their neighbors or take away their territory. They just yearned for excitement, and wanted to take chances, to risk their own scalps and bring home somebody else's.

The Indians of the Southeast tattooed large portions of their bodies, as shown in this painting by Jacques Le Moyne.

Hidden under wolfskins, Indians crept up close to a buffalo herd.

Directly west of the Mississippi a great mixture of tribes lived side by side. Here, Indians were farmers whose cornfields stretched for miles along the river valleys. But the farmers were hunters, too. Besides shooting local game they trekked hundreds of miles to hunt the buffalo on the High Plains. Hunting was a tricky business. The Indians learned to creep up under a wolf skin, for they saw that the buffalo weren't afraid of wolves. They learned to set the prairie on fire to stampede the buffalo over a cliff.

The Mandan of North Dakota were one of the most powerful of these farming tribes. They had 13 villages of round, high-domed lodges made of poles covered with sod. The lodges were quite roomy, but of course, in the winter time the best of windowless houses is apt to get stuffy, especially if dogs share the house with the people. And the Mandan lodges held plenty of dogs. They weren't pets. They earned the right to a place by the fire, for they did the work of horses, as the Indians had no horses at this time.

The travois was the Indians' substitute for a wagon.

When the tribe went on a journey, dogs did the dragging. In winter they were harnessed and pulled toboggans. When there was no snow, two tepee poles would be tied to the dog's shoulders, the free ends of the poles would drag on the ground, and across them a burden would be placed. This was the travois, the Indian's substitute for a wagon. Only fairly small and light loads could be carried by the dogs on the travois. On hunting trips, heavy game, such as buffalo would have to be cut up in small enough sections for the dogs to be able to carry them.

A Mandan earth lodge with high-domed smoke hole.

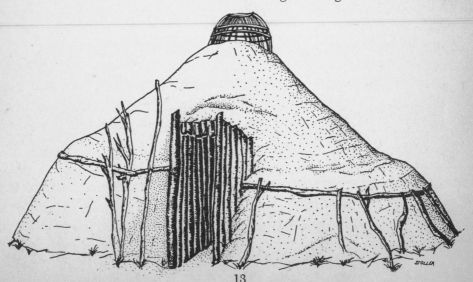

The shirt of this Mandan chief was decorated with the hair of slain enemies.

The Mandans did not depend entirely on the buffalo for their food. They planted maize, beans, pumpkins and sunflowers within the walls of their stockaded villages. They tilled their gardens with planting sticks and hoes fashioned from the shoulder blade of a buffalo.

The Mandan were accomplished potters, and the design and finish of their pottery was exceptionally beautiful. They tempered it by adding sand and grit to make certain it would fire evenly.

The Plains Indians used teepees which could easily be set up during game-hunting expeditions.

This painting shows the interior of a Mandan hut.

The Indians of the Southwest were far removed in their ways as well as in space from the Dakota tribes. When the Spaniards first found Indians living in compact towns of terraced apartment houses built of adobe, they called the Indians "Pueblos," which means "town." The name clung to them, though the real names of the tribes were Zuñi and Hopi. These town-dwelling Indians lived almost entirely by farming and raised many different kinds of corn. But the unusual thing was that here men, not women, worked the fields. There was so little rain in this dry, hot land that farming was very hard work. Moreover, there were no deer to hunt and the Pueblos appeared to have little taste for war.

The Pueblo Indians built their houses several floors high and reached the upper floors by ladders. There was good reason for this, for in time of danger the ladders could be pulled up, preventing anyone from gaining entry. Long before the Pueblos, the cliff dwellers of Mesa Verde and the Grand Canyon built their homes high up on the sides of the canyon walls.

This was a wise precaution, for the fierce Navahos and Apaches who lived near by thought it much easier to raid the hard-working Pueblo

The nomadic Navaho tribes built forked-stick hogans.

16

The Mesa Verde cliff dwellings, built high up on the side of the cliff walls, were built by prehistoric Indian tribes long before white men came to America.

tribes than to work their own land. These two Southwest tribes made war their chief business and lived by raiding other Indian settlements. They were not like the war-loving Indians of the Southeast, however, who went on raids for the excitement of it and who looked forward to running risks and winning glory. The Apaches and Navahos were after booty, and they wanted to get it with as little loss of their own blood as possible. To this end they trained their young men from boyhood to be tough and quick and enduring. They would, for instance, make them run long distances in the heat with their mouths full of water and have them spit out the water afterwards to show they hadn't swallowed it. They were the terror of the region.

Westward beyond the Rockies life was different again. For many of the Indians it was exceedingly hard. Some were so busy searching for food that they had no time for anything else. Certainly not for war. The poorest of all were the Indians of Nevada, whose desert land couldn't be farmed and who were obliged to gather seeds of wild grasses for food and to dig for roots. The early white men called them Diggers. But the Diggers hunted as well as dug. They hunted everything they could find, everything that had life in it—prairie dogs, gophers, rabbits, mice. Nothing was too small for them. They even hunted grasshoppers, digging trenches and driving the insects into them.

The Diggers were constantly on the move, for the land was too poor to support even a small group for very long. They lived in simple sagebrush dwellings, quickly built and soon abandoned. Hunger was their master. It caused them to do things which to us seem cruel but which were for them sheer necessity. When the time came to move and some old person was unable to keep up with the rest of the tribe, he would be abandoned. A little food would be left for the unfortunate one, a little water, and the Indians would go on to the next place that offered seeds and game.

Lodges of the Pima Indians of southern Arizona and northwestern Mexico were built of mud and sticks.

On the Northwest coast the tribes were at the opposite end of the food scale. They had all they wanted to eat without doing any farming, and raised nothing but a little tobacco. They hunted big game—deer and bear, elk and mountain sheep. That was mainly for sport, however. Their chief occupation was fishing. The waters teemed with food—with salmon and smelt, halibut, flounder, and shellfish. The Indians killed porpoises and seals and sea lions. Whales are dangerous prey, but the Nootkas had the courage to go after them, too, and the chief of the tribe himself was the harpooner.

The Northwest coast Indians had not only all the food but also all the wood they wanted. They used wood for everything—to construct their houses, their canoes, their boats. They could make a boat fifty feet long. And they carved everything handsomely, from dishes and spoons and chests and masks and cradles to the totem poles they set up in front of their homes.

The two parts of this mask closed to form the head of a raven.

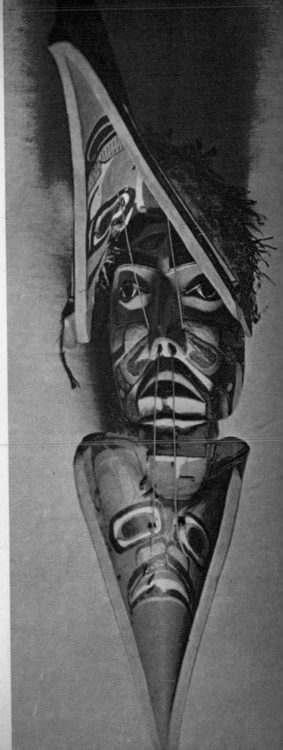

Buffalo Hunt

It was in America that horses developed millions of years ago from tiny creatures no bigger than a fox, to the large, swift-running animals of today. However, for unknown reasons, having got so far, all the horses died out. When the Spaniards brought their horses to the New World, the Indians were terrified of the huge creatures that they had never seen before. But once their terrors were over, how enviously they regarded the white man's horses! The Spaniards, however, guarded their herds, and wherever they pushed their conquest, they forbade Indians to own horses.

Then in 1680 the Pueblo people and the Apaches and Navahos joined forces, rebelled against the Spaniards, and drove them out of Santa Fe. Not for twelve years did the white men return. And in those years the horses ran wild. The Indians got hold of them.

Horses increased on the Plains, and some of the animals that the Spaniards had brought into California escaped up into Oregon. Indians captured them, started horse raising, and traded the animals eastward. The Cayuse Indian tribe were especially shrewd horse traders and *cayuse* became a cowboy word for horse.

Mandan Indians performing the Bull Dance at the start of a buffalo hunt.

21

By the 1700's all the tribes around the buffalo country of the Great Plains got horses and learned to ride. They became marvelous horsemen. And what a difference it made in their hunting! Now, when the huge, heavy buffalo were stampeded over a cliff, the danger of being trampled underfoot was much less when the hunters were on horseback. And with horses instead of dogs to pull the travois, much more meat and many more hides could be carried home. Tribe after tribe changed its way of life to center on the buffalo. The Cheyenne, who had been farmers, forsook their farming. The Blackfoot, the Crow, and many others began to live off buffalo entirely.

The wonderful creature which roamed the Great Plains in tens of millions not only gave the Indians their food—it supplied them with nearly everything else they needed. From the hide they made tepees, clothing, warm bedding, saddles, shields. They used the sinews for bowstrings, for sewing moccasins, leggings, bags. Shoulder bones did duty as hoes, rib bones were turned into runners for dog sleds, porous hip bones became paint brushes. Horns yielded cups and spoons and bowls. Glue was made from the hoofs. Buffalo chips—small pieces of dried dung—were used as fuel. And even the long hair of the buffalo's beard was used in decorations.

There were two great buffalo hunts a year. The major one was held in September when the cows were fat and the wool fresh and thick and good for warm robes. The other hunt was in April, but then only meat and hides were taken. At this time the buffalo were beginning to shed and robes could not be made from their sparse, seedy hair.

The buffalo migrated to the northern plains in spring and down south in the fall, but no one could tell exactly where they might be, for a fire, a flood, a hunt, or a stampede might turn them aside. The Indians often might have to travel anywhere from 150 to 500 miles before they found the herd. All the active members of the tribe left their village, taking their small traveling tepees on the travois.

As the buffalo charged, the Indian plunged his spear.

Scouts were sent on ahead of the hunters. When they had found the buffalo, the rest of the band assembled within a few miles of the herd and made camp. Now, great discipline was observed. No one was permitted to slip out to hunt on his own, for the buffalo might easily be frightened away. Young warriors—members of the Dog Society, like the dancer on page 4—policed the camp, and if they caught anyone going off to hunt, they would lash him with their quirts, cut his robes and his lodge to pieces, and kill his horses.

Sometimes the Indians would stampede the buffalo over the edge of a cliff.

Others waiting below would skin the carcasses and prepare to butcher them.

After surrounding a herd of buffalo, the hunters would cut out the cows from the bulls, as cow meat was considered better eating.

At the start of a hunt, the men streamed out of camp in a body, spirits high, weapons in perfect condition. Each hunter rode some secondary horse, leading his trained buffalo pony to keep it fresh. All rode bareback, and as they neared the buffalo they rode in silence.

The first step was to make the surround, encircling the herd. Spreading out on all sides and using every available man, the Indians rode around the animals. Then at a signal the hunters charged. The startled buffalo milled round and round, sending up a choking dust. But the well-trained horses didn't balk. They seemed to enjoy the sport as they galloped of their own accord beside the speeding buffalo, leaving the hunter's hands free to shoot. Cutting through the bulls, which were not considered good eating, the Indians pursued the swift-running cows and shot down as many as they needed or were able to hit. They killed only the number of animals needed for food and for robes for the coming months. There was no needless slaughter.

Then came the butchering. To save the meat from the hungry wolves that circled the camp, the men worked far on into the night. But long before that the women would have brought up the pack horses and the travois, and the loading would have begun. It was an exciting time, a joyous time, a time when everybody in camp had his fill of fresh meat every day. Even the dogs were royally fed.

It was a time of hard work, too. Back in camp the meat had to be cut into thin sheets and hung high up on scaffolds, out of reach of wolves and dogs, to dry in sun and wind. If it rained, the work was harder still, for the meat could not be allowed to spoil. Great fires of buffalo chips had to be kept going day and night to dry it.

It took many hunts and much work on the part of the women to store up enough food for six months ahead. The meat would be packed like shingles, put on the travois along with the robes, and the homeward journey would begin. Afterwards the meat would be pounded into powder, dried cherries or berries would be added to it, fat or marrow would be poured over all, and the whole would be tightly packed in rawhide cases. This was called pemmican. Pemmican was about as nourishing a thing as you could eat, and it would keep indefinitely.

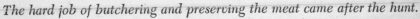

The hard job of butchering and preserving the meat came after the hunt.

Huntsmen returned to their camp with the kill.

Mountain Men

Before 1800, few white men had ventured deep into Indian territory west of the Mississippi River. Then, the first hardy individuals known as "mountain men" entered the area.

These men who went trapping in the Rockies adopted many Indian ways in order to survive in the wilderness. Not only did they need great physical endurance but they also needed all the Indian's alertness, all his animal watchfulness. For by the 1800's the white man in the plains had earned the Indian's hatred. A white man in Indian country seldom went to sleep in his blankets without knowing that he might be killed before morning.

What, then, made the mountain men go off into the Rockies? Beaver took them there, they said. The finest men's hats were being made of beaver, hat makers were clamoring for the pelts and would pay high prices for them.

Jim Baker, one of the early trappers and frontiersmen, dressed in the buckskins and moccasins of an Indian.

After a solitary winter spent in the mountains trapping beaver, the mountain men gathered for a Rendezvous to trade their furs.

The men took little with them, for they lived mainly off their hunting. A rifle, powder and lead, a knife, an awl, a hatchet, a frypan, a coffeepot, tobacco, blankets and traps, a horse, a mule or two.

When streams froze and the beaver retired to his lodge, the mountain man went into his winter quarters, too. He built himself an arched framework of saplings, shaping a wigwam covered with skins. A fire by the open side cooked his food and gave him warmth. In the river bottoms, emptied now of the spring floods, his animals fed on good grass. When snow fell they gnawed the bark from cottonwood boughs he cut for them. Game was plentiful, for buffalo came up from the plains.

In the spring the beaver were at their best, and by summer the mountain men had many a hundred-pound pack of pelts ready to trade. Then off they went to the Rendezvous, or great meeting place.

The Rendezvous was holiday time for the mountain men. They sold their pelts, bought new equipment, and then let loose. There were contests of skill. Men ran and jumped, wrestled, and shot with the rifle. They sang together and laughed and whooped, quarreled and fought. They feasted on hump ribs and had coffee with sugar in it. They gambled and drank whisky and made up for the hardships they had endured.

Then the Rendezvous would be over and the mountain men would start for the Rockies again—no richer than the year before. But there were more beaver in the mountains. Next summer would be different.

For most of them it never was. And soon the whole thing ended. The trappers had trapped too many beaver too fast. There weren't enough left in the Rocky Mountains to make trapping worth while. In exchange for his pelts a man couldn't get even the few things he needed. And besides, the fashion in men's hats had changed, and "beavers" were no longer stylish.

By the 1840's most of the mountain men disappeared, leaving behind only the memory of their skill and of their lonely, daring life.

The mountain men learned to live like Indians, and to know the trails over the wild mountain country as well as the red men. Later, some mountain men became scouts and guides for the early wagon trains that first crossed the country.

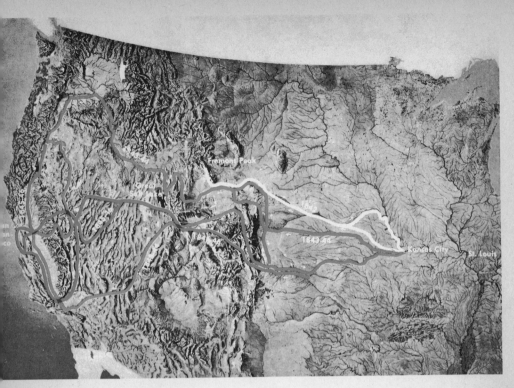

The three expeditions, shown in red, white and blue on the map, made by John Charles Frémont, opened the western territory to white settlers.

A few of the mountain men gave their names to history. Kit Carson was one, who became a guide for John Charles Frémont, the great pathfinder of the West. In 1842 Frémont was sent out to locate the South Pass through the Rockies in order that covered wagons might be driven through to Oregon.

Frémont took Carson with him on two other expeditions—to Oregon and California, and the scout had the explorer's respect all the way.

Frémont wrote such enthusiastic reports of Carson that Kit became a national figure. His very name drew pioneers to follow his path and begin the westward migration which settled the prairie and mountain country in the years that followed.

Snake and Sioux Indians, riding their ponies
bareback, charged on the warpath.

Westward Ho!

The covered wagons came across the prairies, through South Pass, heading for Oregon. The Indians were waiting for them. What right did white men have to trespass on their territory? Who had given them permission to kill game and build forts on their land?

The pioneers had expected Indian trouble, but not like this. They had known only the Indians who lived east of the Mississippi. These daredevils of the Plains were different creatures altogether. They had horses, and on his horse the Plains Indian was a perfect fighting machine. He could drop his body on either side of his mount, hang on by his heels

United States troopers rode along with the supply trains to protect them in hostile Indian territory.

Indians would stampede a buffalo herd through a wagon train in an effort to drive the white men from their lands.

over the horse's back, and screen himself from his enemies' weapons. He tore along, shooting arrows so fast that one or more was in the air all the time. What could a pioneer do against an enemy like that, who could not only shoot eight arrows in the time it took to reload a rifle, but who was also becoming as skillful with guns as white men themselves?

The trail to Oregon was blazed, but it was no pleasure trip. It took five months to trek over the 2,000 miles of plain, mountain, desert, and mountain again. And at any moment hostile Indians might appear. In the buffalo country they might cause the whole herd to stampede and come thundering into the wagon train—a sure way to wreck it.

But still the land-hungry pioneers came on. Thousands braved the journey. Other thousands took the Santa Fe Trail to the rich farmlands of California. When gold was discovered, the "forty-niners" poured across the overland trails.

With only the bow and arrow, the Indian was a danger to white men.

There were forts now all over the West. Soldiers from the forts were supposed to keep the Plains Indians quiet, but their task was not an easy one, for the Indians were aroused. They saw their lands invaded, their game killed, and their treaties broken. Some struck back. They

When he begun to use muskets and rifles, he was a terrifying enemy.

attacked the covered wagons, the overland stage, and the supply trains. The Government wanted to put the Indians on reservations and give them rations, but the Indians wanted their freedom, their way of life, and the buffalo. And in dismay they saw the buffalo passing away.

The East was calling for hides. No matter how many millions were shipped, still the call came for more. Teamsters, cabbies, all the men who worked outside in the cold and wet wanted buffalo coats. The traders put rifles in the hands of the Indians so they could kill more buffalo. White men—buffalo hunters—made a business of killing buffalo just for the hide, and the prairies were strewn with rotting carcasses.

Then came the railroads. The construction gangs had to be fed. Buffalo Bill, one of the best scouts of the time, earned his nickname when he was hired at $500 a month to supply the railroad with hind quarters. He killed 4,280 buffalo for the company. Then the railroads began advertising buffalo hunts. They even ran excursion trains to the feeding grounds so that people might shoot buffalo from train windows.

The Indian's strength and whole way of life depended upon the buffalo.

Troopers were sent to quell Indian uprisings.

When the white men first came to America, there were something like 60 million buffalo. It seemed as if nothing could destroy them. "They are like our great forests," people said. "They will last forever." A migrating herd was said to cover the ground like a carpet.

Now the eyes of the whole shocked world were turned on the Plains where the chief business was killing the buffalo. Never before had wild animals been slaughtered in such numbers. People were alarmed. They wanted the killing stopped. In 1875 Kansas and Colorado passed laws. But it was already too late, for nearly all the buffalo that remained had been driven south into Texas. And in Texas the Army commander, who had had his hands full of Indian trouble, said that the hunters were doing more to settle the Indian question than the entire Army had done in thirty years. They should be given a medal showing a dead buffalo on one side and a discouraged Indian on the other. "Let them kill until the buffalo is exterminated," he said. "Then we'll have peace."

Longhorns and Cowboys

Everyone could see what was going to happen. The buffalo would be killed off, and the starving Indians would go to the reservations.

But meantime something else was happening. Down in Southern Texas there were longhorned cattle. The Spaniards had brought them in long ago, and the animals had prospered as, indeed, was natural, for they had plenty of grass, plenty of water, and a mild climate. The herds had grown so amazingly that by 1866 there were 4 million head. There were so many that they fetched no more than $5 a head.

Now in the East cattle were bringing ten times as much, and even in Kansas and Missouri they were being sold for $30 a head. Some of the Texas cattlemen decided to take a chance, for they heard that at Abilene, Kansas, at the end of the new east-west railroad, a cattle market had been opened. They would drive their cattle up to Abilene and sell the longhorns at the railhead to be shipped east.

So longhorns took the trail to what became the first of the "cow towns." Four million cattle went north in 15 years. The longhorns were hardy. They could go long stretches without water and still be in shape to cross rivers where the bottom was mud or quicksand. The only trouble with the creatures was that they were nervous—they would break away in a mad rush if any little thing frightened them. It took good horsemen and steady nerves and rugged bodies to handle a herd of 3,000 long-

horns. The Texas cowboy came to the fore. He had been roping the wild longhorns for years and he quickly learned the best way to manage cattle on the long drive— keep them safe and together and headed in the right direction.

First, the animals were passed through a wooden chute and given a road brand. Then 12 to 18 men, in pairs, would string the longhorns out in a line that might stretch half a mile. The most experienced cow-

Sheepskin chaps protected the cowboy's legs in brush country, his hat kept off the sun and rain, and his neckerchief kept out the dust.

Sometimes raiding Indians attacked the cattle drives, seeking the remuda that traveled with the cowboys.

boys would be up at the "point" in front, directing the line of march and setting the pace. Next came the "swing." Then came the "flank." The last in the line were the "dragmen," and they had the worst place, for all the lame and lazy cattle were there. "Bringing in the drag" meant prodding the weaklings and having to ride through the dust screen kicked up by cattle in the lead. Fellows who were learning had to take on that job.

The herd was moved slowly at first because the cattle had to be "road-broken," and fifteen miles a day was as fast as they could go.

When everything was going smoothly and the cowboys were just riding along crooning a tune to keep the cattle quiet, it didn't seem as if being a cowboy called for any special talent. But there was tension all the way. A hailstorm, a flash of lightning, a flock of prairie chickens suddenly flying up might set the cattle off in a mad stampede. And the six-shooters hanging from the cowboys' belts were there for a purpose. Indian raiders might turn up at any time. Mainly, the Indians were after the "remuda," the band of extra horses, but they stampeded the cattle to cause confusion and to get what they wanted. White rustlers were worse. They generally came at night, stampeded the cattle and drove off part of the herd to some fastness in the hills. Two cowboys had to ride around the herd all night long to guard it. Sometimes for a week everybody slept with his boots on, ready to spring into the saddle.

But whether the herd stampeded or not, the long drive was a strain, and by the time the cattle reached the end of the trail, were turned over to the new owner and packed into cattle cars, the cowboys were ready for a good time. They had been working from before dawn to after dark, eighteen hours a day. Now they let loose. They behaved just like the mountain men at their Rendezvous—drank and gambled and danced.

Cowboys waved a saddle blanket or shot their six-guns in the air, to herd stray cattle back into line.

Before long, Texas cattlemen realized that cattle could be raised cheaply in other places beside Texas. Millions of buffalo had grazed on the plains. Cattle would thrive there, too.

So a new method of cattle raising was developed. Cattle were bred in Texas and the Southwest and then driven as young steers to the central and northern Plains. The whole region where the buffalo had roamed and Indians had hunted became one huge cattle range. Cattle were raised from Texas all the way to Canada.

The Overland stage ran from Missouri to California.

Drivers were always prepared for an attack by hostile Indians.

With the coming of the railroad, the Indian knew his days of freedom on the plains were coming to an end.

The land had belonged to the Indians, but the Indians couldn't withstand armies, nor could they hold out against starvation. Now, their home became government land, free grazing land, free for anyone's cattle.

The buffalo were almost gone. An iron road cut through the prairie where the great hunts had taken place. The Indians stared at the rails and knew that the joyous, free life of the Plains was over. Telegraph wires were strung across the lands, carrying reports of Indian uprisings faster than any Indian scout could travel. Many yielded to the pressure of the white men, gave up the lands for which they had fought, and went to live on reservations. But the struggle between white man and Indian was not yet ended. Much blood would be spilled before all the Plains Indians would finally give up their homeland.

The greatest storm center was up in the north where lived the most powerful of the Sioux tribes—the Dakotas. They had been great raiders in their day, had fought other Indian tribes and done more than their share of attacking wagon trains. Now they were ready for peace. Hard experience had taught them that no resistance they could put up would stop the westward trek—they could fight the white man's wagon trains but not his armies. All the Indians asked for now was to be let alone, to be allowed to live in their own way. If the white men would stay away from them, there would be peace, they said.

In 1868 the United States signed a treaty with the Dakotas. The country north of the North Platte was to be theirs forever and no person should ever be permitted to pass over or settle on their land. But like

Telegraph wires which were strung across the prairie by the 1880's hastened the final defeat of the Indian nations.

every other treaty the Government had made with the Indians, this treaty, too, was soon broken.

The reason was gold. Rumors had sprung up that the precious yellow metal was to be found in the Black Hills location of the Sioux. Excited prospectors stole in, a few at a time at first, more and more as the gold fever spread. The Sioux protested. Then the Army stepped in, seized the miners, and turned them over to a court. But not one was found guilty. So they all came back and brought more with them.

"We'll buy mining rights from you," the Government proposed to the angry Indians, "for $6,000,000."

The Dakotas laughed at the offer. More than that had already been taken out of the Black Hills, they said. If the Great Father wanted to buy their land and get rich, they wanted to be made rich, too. They would not settle for less than 50 million dollars.

Railroads further opened the West, not only to white settlers but also to buffalo hunters who came in great numbers from the East.

Custer's Last Stand was one of the last, and most famous of the Indian rebellions against the white man's encroachment on Indian lands.

"The Government will have to show its power," people said impatiently. "That's the only way to make the Indians change their mind."

So an order went out—the Indians would all have to come in and be "enrolled." Most of the bands obeyed, but Sitting Bull, the powerful old Sioux medicine man, and Chief Crazy Horse would not. They understood what was behind the order, and Sitting Bull sent back word: "I have no land to sell. We don't want any white men here."

A second order went out. If Sitting Bull and Crazy Horse didn't come in, the Army would take action against them.

"You can find me easily," Sitting Bull returned. "I will not run away."

The Government sent in General George A. Custer to strike the Indians—and everybody knows what happened then. At the Battle of the Little Big Horn the united Sioux and Cheyenne wiped out Custer's troops to a man.

General George A. Custer.

The news of that defeat rocked the nation. People called it a massacre. Only a few kept their heads, saying, "We asked for it. Custer was going in to get them and they got him first. Every time we wipe out an Indian village and kill every man, woman, and child we call that a great victory. When the Indians do the same thing to us, we call it a massacre."

Sitting Bull and Crazy Horse had won the greatest triumph the Indians had ever had over the white man. But they didn't want to keep on fighting—they knew the power against them was too strong. After terrible suffering, Crazy Horse and his band laid down their arms. The Chief had been promised that not a hair of his head would be touched. But this promise was broken, and he died fighting to escape the shameful death awaiting him.

"They say we massacred Custer," he said before he died. "But he would have done the same to us. We wanted to escape, but we were so hemmed in we had to fight."

Chief Sitting Bull

52

Sitting Bull and his Dakotas retreated to Canada. Canada, however, didn't want them, and the Indians drifted back to the reservation. When the old medicine man finally laid down his arms, many people wanted him to be executed as a common criminal, but others said, "He never wanted war. He and his people were goaded into battle."

Soon after the Custer affair, more Indian trouble broke out, this time in the far northwest. There where the corners of Oregon, Washington, and Idaho meet, lived the Nez Percés, an intelligent and peaceful group of Indians. When the white men put pressure on them to move, their great leader, Chief Joseph, persuaded them to accept life on a reservation. But the white men wanted everything.

"We will not give up our homeland," said the young men.

They fought—magnificently—but they were hopelessly outnumbered. The women and children going with the warriors, the tribe marched away over the mountains towards Canada in one of the great retreats of military history. All the way—for four months and 1,300 miles—they fought with the troops sent to pursue them. Almost in sight of the Canadian border, worn out and near starvation, the Indians were trapped and surrounded. Chief Joseph, one of the greatest of Indian generals, made a last desperate stand. Then when honorable terms were offered him, he surrendered.

For many years Geronimo, one of the most famous Apache chieftains, led the final struggle against the white man on the United States-Mexican border. He is shown here (center) just before his final surrender in 1886.

Chief Joseph, who led the Nez Percés Indians in their last struggle against the white man in a heroic 1,300 mile retreat. Below, the courageous Indian chieftain surrenders the Nez Percés to government troops.

"I am tired of fighting," he told the white officers. "Our chiefs are killed. . . . It is cold and we have no blankets. The little children are freezing to death. My people—have run away to the hills and have no blankets, no food. . . . I want to have time to look for my children and see how many I can find. . . . Hear me, my chiefs. I am tired; my heart is sick and sad. From where the sun now stands, I will fight no more forever."

Chief Joseph had won the admiration and the warm liking of his white opponents. But immediately after his surrender, the promises made to him were broken. He and all his people were shipped to Oklahoma, where many of them died of heat and low altitude and heartbreak.

As for Sitting Bull, Buffalo Bill got him to join his Wild West Show along with a lot of other Dakotas, and the old Indian toured the United States and Europe. Everywhere he went he made speeches calling for peace and understanding of his people. Finally he tired of the curious crowds who wanted to buy his autograph and came back to the reservation, only to be murdered in the end by the authorities.

The last great flares of Indian revolt were now extinguished and three noble Indian leaders had passed from the scene. But Sitting Bull and Crazy Horse, at least, continued to live on in the American imagination. For they had packed the word *Sioux* with unforgettable excitement. *Sioux* made the white man think of war-whoops and scalps and daredevil riders scooping up their dead and wounded from the ground. Today the word is still packed with excitement. But it brings to mind much more than merciless fighting. *Sioux* calls up the whole vanished life of the Plains and brings back the spirit of the Old West.

PICTURE CREDITS